William Giffe

Crown of gold

For Sunday-schools

William Giffe

Crown of gold
For Sunday-schools

ISBN/EAN: 9783337269296

Printed in Europe, USA, Canada, Australia, Japan

Cover: Foto ©Paul-Georg Meister /pixelio.de

More available books at **www.hansebooks.com**

FOR

SUNDAY-SCHOOLS, GOSPEL SERVICES,
REVIVAL MEETINGS, CHRISTIAN ENDEAVOR
SOCIETIES, EPWORTH LEAGUES, Etc.

BY

W. T. GIFFE and FRANK M. DAVIS.

Published by
THE HOME MUSIC CO.,
LOGANSPORT, IND.

PREFACE.

Within this enclosure lie
Fragrant fields of poesy and song.
Between the rhymes, in soft and gentle cadence,
Flow beautiful streams of living thought,
Pure and refreshing:
On their banks you may sit and
Twine in wreaths of sacred melody
Your heart's devotion to Christ.
As you sing you may feel
The glory of God's unspeakable love,
In the sunshine of which there is
Sweet peace.

    We will not detain you further
    At the gateway.
    Lift the latch and
    Pass in.

                                                  THE AUTHORS.

CAUTION.—Nearly all the words and music in "Crown of Gold" are copyright property. All rights of republication of the words or music, separate or combined, are reserved and will be defended by the owners of the copyright.

Crown of Gold copyrighted MDCCCXCII, by The Home Music Co.

THE CHILDREN FOR JESUS. Concluded.

No. 3. GOD'S EYE WATCHES.
W. A. O.   W. A. O.

No. 4, WATCHMAN OF ZION.
Milo W. Nethercutt.

6

SINGING SONGS FOR JESUS. Concluded.

No. 9. NIGHT HYMN.

Jay P.   Jay Powell.

1. Dark-ness falls up-on our pathway, Nature's eyes are closed in sleep;
2. Light in dark-ness, joy in sor-row, Peace in trou-ble, love in fear;
3. Thus our days are filled with gladness, Thus our nights de-void of gloom,

Phantom ships in noise-less mo-tion Rock up-on the qui-et deep.
These the fruits of thy sweet spir-it, Nought a-larms when thou art near.
Though perchance a touch of sad-ness, Comes, en-rich-ing love's per-fume.

CHORUS.

Gra-cious Fa-ther, guard our slumbers, May our wak-ing thoughts be pure;

Pure be-cause these frail clay ves-sels Rest-ed in thine arms se-cure.

BEYOND THE BLUE. Concluded.

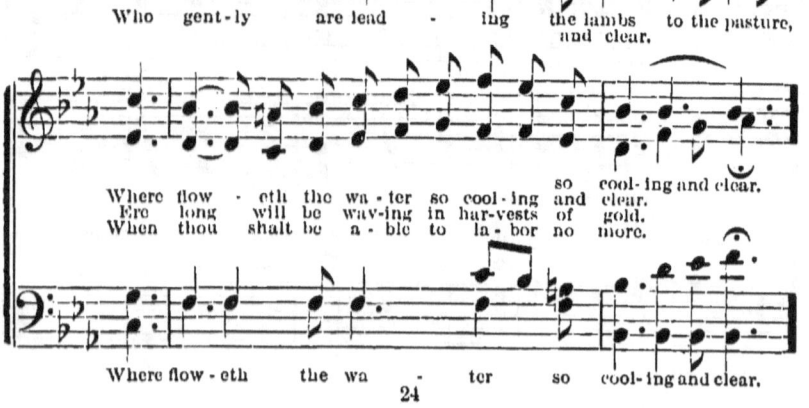

THOU SHALT SHINE. Concluded.

No. 24. WE'VE BEEN REDEEMED.

Mrs. M. J. Cartwright.   W. T. Giffe.

1. We've been re-deemed, my broth-er, O, hear the joy-ful news; Such
2. I've been re-deemed, my broth-er, My Sav-ior now is near; To
3. I'm glad I've come to Je-sus, He'll cleanse my ev-ery stain; For

won-der-ful sal-va-tion You sure-ly won't re-fuse.
me he's gen-tly saying These words of hope and cheer.
nev-er wea-ry wand'rer has sought his face in vain.

CHORUS.

Come ... un-to me,   Je - sus is call-ing,   Come ... un-to me,   I will keep you from fall-ing.
Come un-to me,   Je-sus now is ten-der-ly call-ing, Come un-to me, Come un-to me,

HOLD THOU MY HAND. Concluded.

Hold thou my hand, O Father, Hold thou my hand, I pray,
When shad-ows fall a-bout me And hide the beat-en way.

No. 26. A LAST PRAYER.

HELEN HUNT JACKSON.
(Four days before her death.)

W. T. GIFFE.

1. Fa-ther, I scarce-ly dare to pray, So clear I see, now it is done,
2. So clear I see the things I thought Were right or harmless, were a sin;
3. In out-skirts of thy king-dom vast, Fa-ther, the humblest spot give me;

That I have wast-ed half my day, And left my work but just be-gun.
So clear I see that I have sought, Un-conscious, selfish aims to win.
Set me the low-liest task thou hast, Let me, repentant, work for thee.

No. 28. DO THY LITTLE.

CHAS. EDW. POLLOCK.

THE BEAUTIFUL HILLS. Concluded.

thrill of im-mor-tal eyes, In the night of our dark-est woe.
bur-den which they did then, Nor shrink from their thorny crown.
God on our lives will play, Till our bod-ies bloom to souls

CHORUS.

Then sing for the beau-ti-ful hills, That rise from the bright hills, ev-er-green-shore; O, sing for the beau-ti-ful green shore, hills, Where the wea-ry shall toil no more. bright hills.

No. 30. FATHER, TAKE ME BY THE HAND.

Rev. J. B. Smith.   E. S. Rice.

1. Take me by the hand, my Father, For I do not know the way; Night shades round me quickly gather, Hold me, else I go astray. Many are the ills betiding Those who tread the way alone; Many are the foes con-

2. Toilsome is the way I'm treading, Hard and rough the dizzy height; Heavy are the mists o'erspreading, And my home is out of sight. When I'm death's dark valley nearing, And approach the untried land, With the judgment day ap-

FATHER, TAKE ME. Concluded.

37

THROUGH THE BLOOD. Concluded.

Do you hope for heav-en Thro' the blood of the Christ cru-ci-fied?

No. 32. THOU ART MY SHEPHERD.

M. E. THALHEIMER.   J. CRAMER.

1. Thou art my shep-herd, Car-ing for all my need, Thy lit-tle lamb to feed, Trusting thee still. In the green pastures low, Where liv-ing wa-ters flow, Safe by thy side I go, Fear-ing no ill.

2. If thou wilt guide me, Glad-ly I'll go with thee; No harm can come to me, Holding thy hand. And soon my wea-ry feet, Safe in the gold-en street, Where all who love thee meet, Re-deemed shall stand.

LET YOUR LIGHT SHINE. Concluded.

Let your light . . shine, brightly shine . . .
trav'ler in the night; Let your light shine, let your light bright-ly shine.

No. 34.   SOME SWEET DAY.

S. H. C.   S. H. Chord.

1. Some sweet day when life is o'er, We shall meet a-bove,
2. Tri - als here be - low we meet, Sor-row, pain and care,
3. Bright the dawn-ing of that morn, Night be turned to day,

We shall greet those gone be - fore, In that home of love.
In that hap - py home so sweet, Joy and peace we'll share.
Part - ed friends no fare-wells know, Tears be wiped a - way.

REFRAIN.

Some sweet day, some sweet day, Oh! that happy time will be, some sweet day.

STAND LIKE THE BRAVE. Concluded.

No. 36. GOD HOLDS THE KEY.

J. H. Fillmore.

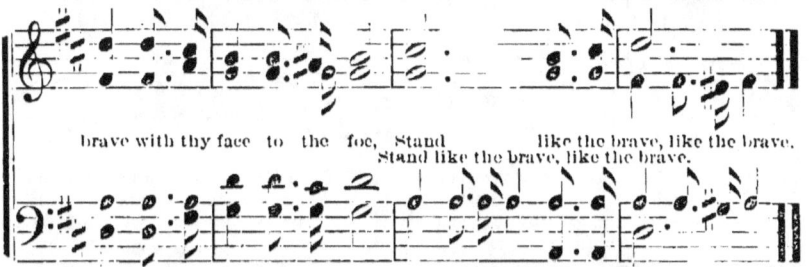

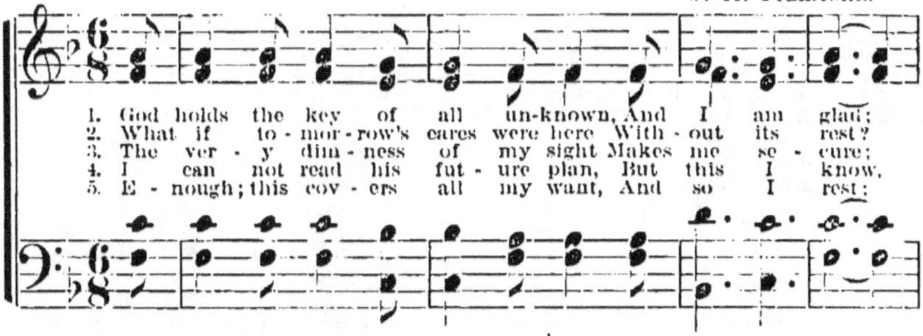

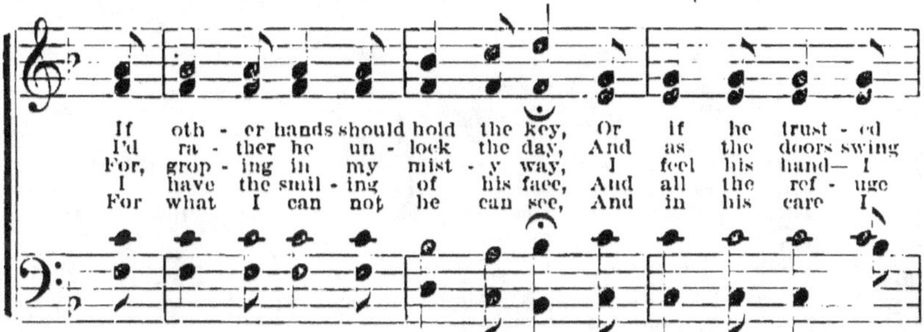

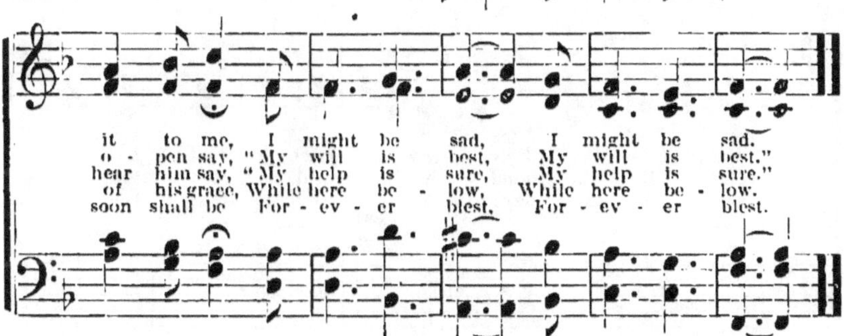

SALVATION BELLS. Concluded.

No. 40. MY SHEPHERD LEADS.

W. F. McNamara. W. T. Giffe.

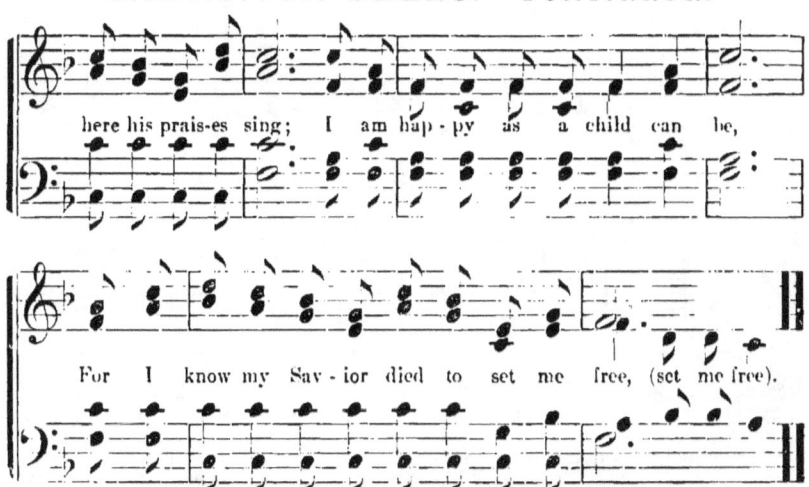

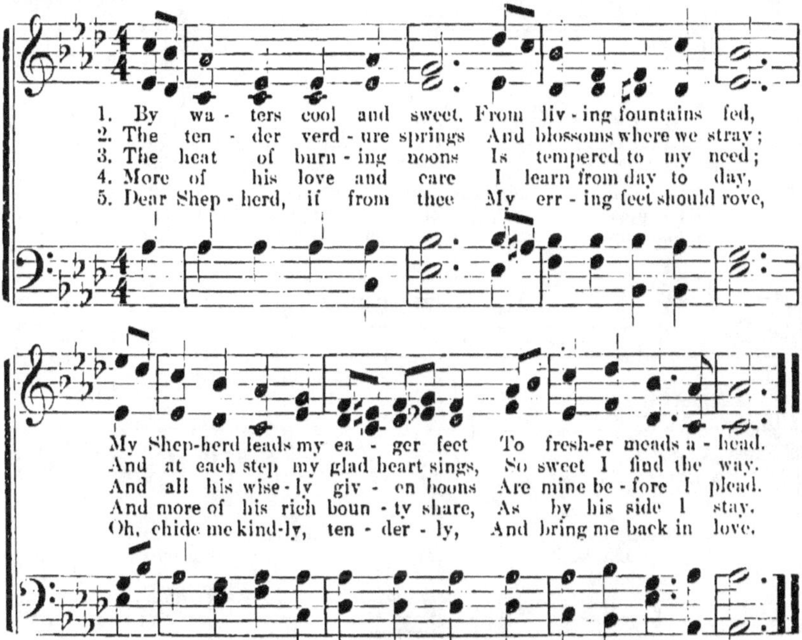

WHEN WE ALL GET HOME. Concluded.

Repeat *pp* last time.

Ev - er praise . . the Lord, When we all get home.
Ev - er praise the Lord, When we all get home.

No. 42. ABIDE WITH ME.

H. F. LYTE. Arr. by W. H. MONK.

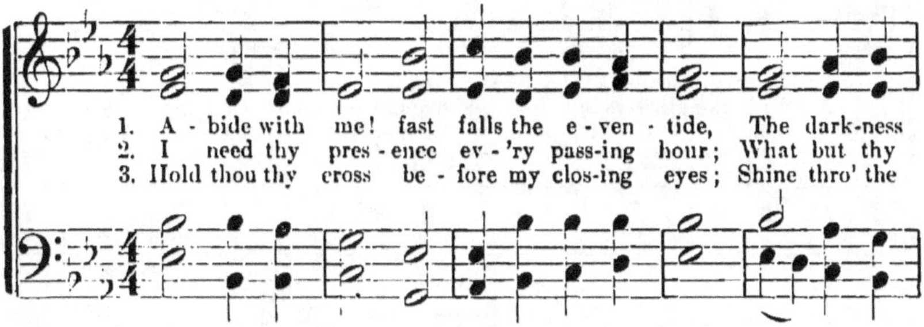

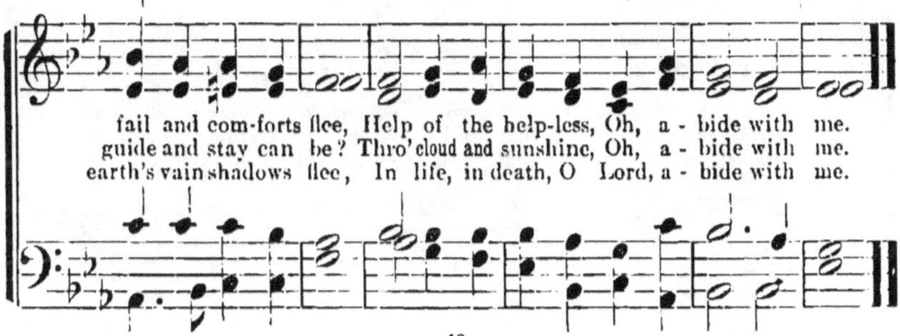

1. A - bide with me! fast falls the e - ven - tide, The dark-ness deep - ens; Lord, with me a - bide! When oth - er help - ers fail and com-forts flee, Help of the help-less, Oh, a - bide with me.
2. I need thy pres - ence ev - 'ry pass-ing hour; What but thy grace can foil the tempter's pow'r? Who like thy - self my guide and stay can be? Thro' cloud and sunshine, Oh, a - bide with me.
3. Hold thou thy cross be - fore my clos-ing eyes; Shine thro' the gloom, and point me to the skies; Heav'n's morning breaks and earth's vain shadows flee, In life, in death, O Lord, a - bide with me.

No. 43. HEAVEN ENOUGH FOR ME.

M. M. L.
M. M. Luzader. Arr. by W. T. G.

1. When I reach the gold-en shore be-yond the sea, (o - ver there),
2. I'll go march-ing down the streets all paved with gold, (o - ver there),
3. There I'll sing re-deem-ing love that saved my soul, (o - ver there),

When the beau-ti-ful gates shall swing a-jar for me (o - ver there);
With the glit-ter-ing, hap-py throng I soon shall be (o - ver there);
What a glo-ri-ous song of tri-umph that will be (o - ver there);

As I pass the por-tals bright and fair, my song then shall be,
All my loved ones gone be-fore I soon shall find o - ver there.
From his place up-on the throne he'll cast a smile down on me.

I'm re-deemed! Oh, that will be heav'n e-nough for me.
Praise the Lord! Oh, that will be heav'n e-nough for me.
Praise the Lord! Oh, that will be heav'n e-nough for me.

HEAVEN ENOUGH FOR ME. Concluded.

No. 44. OUR JEWELS.

Rev. G. W. Crofts.   Frank M. Davis.

1. Heav'n is gath'ring up our jewels, Brightest jewels that we own; There they shine in wondrous splendor, Adding lus-ter to its throne.
2. As we look may we not see them, Like the stars of ev'ning shine, Far a-bove these earthly shadows, In their beauty all di-vine.
3. There no harm shall ev-er reach them, Nor the burden of a sigh; Sorrows shall not gather 'round them, Like the clouds that veil the sky.

CHORUS.

Christ is com-ing, Christ is com-ing, Gath'ring up his pre - cious gems, Plac-ing them to shine for-ev-er, . . . In his royal di-a-dems.
Christ is coming, Christ is com-ing, He's gath'ring up his precious gems, them to shine for - ev-er, for-ev-er, roy - al di-a-dems.

No. 47. ANYWHERE MY SAVIOR LEADS.

BRING BEAUTIFUL LILIES. Concluded.

No. 53. HAPPY THOUGHTS.

Selected by LAURA RICHARDS.   C. V. STRICKLAND.

W. C. T. U. SONG. Concluded.

monster from the land, That we in safe-ty once a-gain may dwell.

No. 55. COME, LITTLE ONE.

R. A. EVILSIZER. W. T. GIFFE.

1. Come, lit-tle one, with your even-ing pray'r, Kneel-ing so
2. Pray for a heart that is clean and pure, Pray for a
3. Ask him to bless ev'-ry good true friend, Ask him to

low at your moth-er's chair; Come, meek-ly clasp-ing your
love that is strong and sure; Pray to be gen-tle and
keep you un-til the end; Trust in his kind-ness and

dim-pled hands, Je-sus loves chil-dren and un-der-stands.
good and true, Ask for his bless-ing to rest on you.
love, dear child, Je-sus, the Christ-child, was meek and mild.

No. 59. BEAUTIFUL HOME-LAND.

Jessie H. Brown.   Milo W. Nethercutt.

1. Beau-ti-ful home-land, home of the blest, Sweet is thy mu-sic, calm is thy rest; Oft-en I whis-per, dream-ing of thee,
2. Crown of re-joic-ing, crown of the pure, To-ken of glo-ry end-less and sure; Oft-en I whis-per, dream-ing of thee,
3. Glo-ri-fied Sav-ior, Sav-ior di-vine, Thou hast re-deemed me, now I am thine; Oft-en I whis-per, lean-ing on thee,

CHORUS.

Beau-ti-ful home-land, art thou for me?   Beau-ti-ful home-land,
Crown of re-joic-ing, art thou for me?   Beau-ti-ful home-land,
Glo-ri-fied Sav-ior, thou art for me!

Beau-ti-ful home of the soul, Beau-ti-ful home-land, Shall I be there?
fade - less and fair;

No. 61. GATHER THE LOST ONES IN.

E. R. LATTA. FRANK M. DAVIS.

1. Gath-er the lost ones in, Wan-der-ing here and there,
2. Gath-er the lost ones in, Gath-er the young and old;
3. Gath-er the lost ones in, Think of the beasts of prey;
4. Gath-er the lost ones in, Gath-er from all a-larms

Down in the deep ra-vines Or on the mountains bare.
Shel-ter them ere the night, Safe in the Shep-herd's fold.
Some of the flock are safe, What of the part a-stray?
In-to the fold of love, In-to the Sav-ior's arms.

CHORUS.

Gath - - er them in, ... Out of the haunts of sin, Gather them
Gather them in, gather them in,

in, ... Whithersoever they've been, Gather the lost ones in.
Gather them in, gather them in,

No. 62. CHRISTIAN BATTLE SONG.

W. T. G.
With enthusiasm.
W. T. Giffe.

1. Send a shout a-long the line, Re-in-force-ments com-ing! 'Round Im-man-uel's ban-ner See them bravely thronging. Fierce the bat-tle ra-ges, Strong the hosts of sin; But our great Com-mand-er Will the vic-t'ry win.
2. See, the foe is fal-t'ring now! Truth has van-quished er-ror! Foiled are Satan's for-ces, Back they fly in ter-ror. Forward now, my broth-ers, Shout it down the line! Re-in-force-ments com-ing! See their ar-mor shine! Shout! shout the vic-to-ry, Vic-t'ry o-ver sin;
3. Lift your heads, ye gold-en gates, Comes the King of glo-ry! All ye hap-py an-gels, Join to tell the sto-ry, Je-sus, our Re-deem-er, Tri-umphs o-ver sin. Ring the bells of heav-en, Glo-ry be to Him!

Fine. CHORUS. D. S. *Long and fierce the con-flict,*

D. S.

But the right will win.

THE VOYAGE OF LIFE. Concluded.

No. 65. DOVES TO THEIR WINDOWS.

W. A. O.
W. A. OGDEN.

Effective as a Solo.

1. As doves to their windows we're coming to thee, The mer-it of Je-sus our hope and our plea; Dear Fa-ther in heaven, our bur-den of sin We long to lay down and the new life be-gin.
2. As doves to their windows our spir-its would fly, And car-ry our wants to the courts up on high, We plead the dear prom-ise of Je-sus to-day, Oh! Fa-ther in heaven, have mercy, we pray.
3. As doves to their windows, and thou wilt re-ceive, The pray'rs which we of-fer, the hearts we now give; Cre-ate them a-new, let there never more be One thought or de-sire dis-loy-al to thee.

Rit. - - - CHORUS.

Coming, . . we're com-ing, to thee, to thee, Fa-ther in heav-en, we're com-ing to thee, Give us thy spir-it

DOVES TO THEIR WINDOWS. Concluded.

to wit-ness with-in, And we shall be free from our bur-den of sin.

No. 66. CHILDREN'S PRAISES.

English.

1. Once was heard the song of chil-dren, By the Sav-ior when on earth,
2. Palms of vic-t'ry strewn a-round him, Garments spread be-neath his feet,
3. God o'er all the heav-ens reigning, We this day thy glo-ry sing,

Joy-ful in the sa-cred tem-ple, Shouts of youth-ful praise had birth,
Proph-et of the Lord they crowned him, In fair Sa-lem's crowded street,
Not with palms thy path-way strew-ing, We would loft-ier trib-ute bring,

And ho-san-nas, glad ho-san-nas, Loud to Da-vid's Son broke forth.
And ho-san-nas, glad ho-san-nas, From the lips of chil-dren greet.
And ho-san-nas, glad ho-san-nas, We would raise to Christ our King.

NOTHING FURTHER I NEED. Concluded.

No. 68. SABBATH SONG.

M. J. CARTWRIGHT.   W. G. THOMAS.

BLESSED JESUS. Concluded.

keep all my Lord's com-mands; Bless-ed Je - sus, take my hand.

No. 70. CHRISTMAS MORNING.

HENRY A. LEWIS.

1. Lit - tle chil-dren, can you tell, Do you know the sto - ry well,
2. Yes, we know the sto - ry well; List-en now, and hear us tell.
3. Shepherds sat up - on the ground, Fleec-y flocks were scat-tered round,
4. Joy and peace the an-gels sang, And the pleas-ant ech - oes rang,
5. For a lit - tle babe that day—Christ, the Lord of an-gels—lay,

Ev - 'ry girl and ev - 'ry boy—Why the an-gels sang for joy,
Ev - 'ry girl and ev - 'ry boy, Why the an-gels sang for joy,
When the brightness filled the sky, And the song was heard on high,
Peace on earth, to men good will:" Hark! the an - gels sing it still,
Born on earth our Lord to be; This the wond'ring an - gels see,

On a Christ - mas morn - ing? On a Christ - mas morn - ing?

Copyright, 1892, by HENRY A. LEWIS.

No. 78. WE SHOULD HEAR THE ANGELS.

W. T. Giffe.

1. If we on-ly sought to brighten Ev-'ry pathway dark with care,
2. If we on-ly strive to cher-ish Ev-'ry pure and ho-ly thought,
3. If we on-ly did our du-ty, Thinking not what it might cost,

If we on-ly tried to light-en All the burdens others bear.
Till with-in our hearts should per-ish All that is with ev-il fraught.
Then the earth would wear new beau-ty, Like to that in E-den lost.

CHORUS.

We should hear the an-gels singing, All around us night and day, night and day,

We should feel them gen-tly wing-ing, At our side their upward way.

SAFE IN THE FOLD. Concluded.

CHORUS.

Safe, ... safe, ... safe in the fold.
Safe in the fold, safe in the fold,

No. 80. HEAVEN IS MY HOME.

Frank M. Davis.

1. I'm but a stran-ger here, Heav'n is my home; Earth is a des-ert drear, Heav'n is my home. Dan-ger and sor-row stand Round me on ev'ry hand, Heav'n is my fa-ther-land, Heav'n is my home.
2. What though the tem-pest rage, Heav'n is my home; Short is my pil-grimage, Heav'n is my home. Time's cold and win-t'ry blast Soon will be o-ver-past, I shall reach home at last, Heav'n is my home.
3. There at my Sav-ior's side, Heav'n is my home; I shall be glo-ri-fied, Heav'n is my home. There are the good and blest, Those I loved most and best; There, too, I soon shall rest, Heav'n is my home.

THE BEAUTIFUL LAND. Concluded.

VICTORY MARCH. Concluded.

sto - ry, Tell-ing the sto - ry of Jesus...
sto - ry, on-ward,

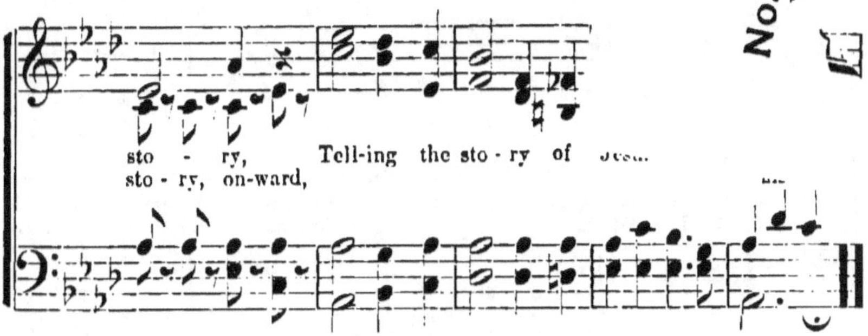

No. 83. I KNOW IT IS THERE.

"Written in the Lamb's book of life."—Rev. 21: 27.

FRANK M. DAVIS.   FRANK M. DAVIS.

1. I re - joice now to know that my sins are for - giv'n, That my
2. Je - sus saved me from sin and from all earth-ly strife, And has
3. Glo - ry be to the Lamb that for sin-ners was slain! He has

REFRAIN.

name's on the book kept by an - gels in heav'n.
writ - ten my name in the Lamb's book of life. Yes, I know it is
writ - ten my name as one cleansed from all stain.

there on those pa - ges so fair, Writ - ten there, writ - ten there.

KNOCKING AT THE DOOR. Concluded.

No. 86. NOTHING LEFT UNDONE.

E. R. Latta. O. M. Livengood.

Not too fast.

1. Was there an-y thing that Je-sus Left un-done, left un-done,
2. Hear him in the gar-den, say-ing: Not my will, not my will;
3. See him now be-trayed by Ju-das To his foes, to his foes;
4. See the crown up-on his fore-head, Thorn-y crown! thorn-y crown!
5. See him on the cross sus-pend-ed, Ag-o-ny! ag-o-ny!

When he came to earth to save us Ev-'ry one, ev-'ry one?
Oh, it was an aw-ful mis-sion To ful-fill, to ful-fill.
All the ter-rors that a-wait him Well he knows, well he knows.
How the ten-der flesh it pierc-es, Press-ing down, press-ing down!
It was all that he might res-cue Such as we, such as we.

CHORUS.

Oh, no! no! no! there was noth-ing left un-done;

Repeat Chorus pp

Oh, no! no! no! there was noth-ing left un-done.

No. 87. SPEAK LOVING WORDS.

Mrs. M. B. Goodwin.   Ora M. Livengood.

1. Speak lov-ing words to wait-ing souls, Speak words of hope and cheer;
2. Speak lov-ing words though sin-ners fail The path of life to find;
3. Speak lov-ing words, for soon thou'lt be Pale, sil-ent and un-known;

Lift up the spir-it bow'd with care, Wipe a-way the mourner's tear.
Point to the way that up-ward leads, Speak words both true and kind.
And lov-ing words a-lone will tell The good that thou hast done.

CHORUS.

Speak lov-ing words, Speak kind-ly words, Speak words of hope and cheer,

Lift up the spir-it bow'd with care, Wipe a-way the mourner's tear.

LET ME CLING TO THY HAND. Concluded.

Be the Rock where I stand, And the shad-ow to cov-er my soul.

No. 90. I WOULD LIVE LIKE JESUS.

R. S. Hanna.   R. S. Hanna.

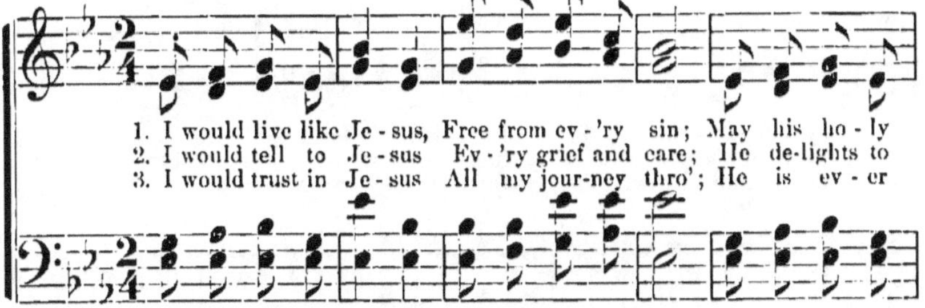

1. I would live like Je-sus, Free from ev-'ry sin; May his ho-ly
2. I would tell to Je-sus Ev-'ry grief and care; He de-lights to
3. I would trust in Je-sus All my jour-ney thro'; He is ev-er

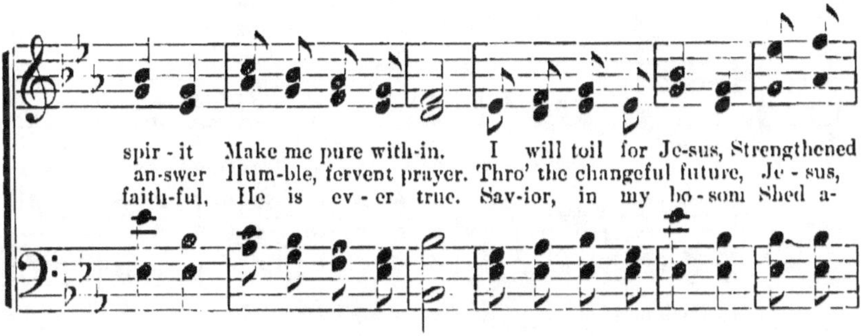

spir-it Make me pure with-in. I will toil for Je-sus, Strengthened
an-swer Hum-ble, fervent prayer. Thro' the changeful future, Je-sus,
faith-ful, He is ev-er true. Sav-ior, in my bo-som Shed a-

by his grace, Till, in end-less glo-ry, I be-hold his face.
be my guide; In thy great compassion, Keep me near thy side.
broad thy love; When I die re-ceive me To thy home a-bove.

WE'LL GATHER. Concluded.

foot-steps may stray (may stray,) The beau-ti-ful, del-i-cate blossoms (the blossoms,) That cheer us, tho' dreary the day (the day.)

No. 94. THERE IS REST IN JESUS.

FRANK M. DAVIS.

1. Come with all thy sor-row, Weary, wand'ring soul; Come to him who loves thee,
2. He thy strength in weak-ness Will thy ref-uge be; Cast on him thy burden,
3. Come in faith be-liev-ing, To his will re-signed; Ask and he will give thee,
4. See the door of mer-cy! Wouldst thou enter there? Knock and he will o-pen,

CHORUS. 1st time. 2d time.

He will make thee whole. { There is rest in Jesus, } Sweet, sweet rest,
He will care for thee.   { There is rest in Jesus, }   Sweet, sweet rest.
Seek and thou shalt find.
Lo, the key is prayer.

WOND'ROUS KING. Concluded.

107

CHRISTIAN WAR SONG. Concluded.

CHORUS.

We march a-long with mer-ry song, And fling our ban-ner high in air,
That all may see what faith are we, Who feel a heav'n-ly Fa-ther's care.
a Fa - ther's care.

No. 99. LOVING JESUS.

W. T. GIFFE.

1. Lov-ing Je-sus, gen-tle lamb, In thy gracious hands I am;
2. I shall then show forth thy praise, Serve thee all my hap-py days;

Make me, Sav-ior, what thou art; Live thy-self with-in my heart.
Then the world shall al-ways see Christ, the ho-ly child, in me.

LET US FORWARD MARCH. Concluded.

march a-long, Sing-ing loud our bat-tle song.
bat-tle song.

No. 105. REMEMBER ME.
Frank M. Davis.

1. When storms a-round are sweeping, When low my watch I'm keep-ing;
2. When walk-ing on life's o-cean, Con-trol its rag-ing mo-tion;
3. When weight of sin op-press-es, When dark de-spair dis-tress-es;

'Mid fires of e-vil fall-ing, 'Mid tempter's voic-es call-ing.
When from its dang-er shrinking, And in its dread deeps sink-ing.
All thro' the life that's mor-tal, And when I pass death's port-al.

REFRAIN.

Re-mem-ber me, O, might-y one, Remember, re-mem-ber me.
remember me.

NO NIGHT IN GLORY. Concluded.

No night in glo-ry! But glo-rious and ne'er-end-ing day!

No. 107.   CORONATION.   C. M.

Ed. Perronet.   Oliver Holden.

1. All hail the pow'r of Je-sus' name! Let an-gels prostrate fall;
2. Let ev-'ry kin-dred, ev-'ry tribe, On this ter-res-trial ball,
3. Oh, that, with yonder sa-cred throng, We at his feet may fall!

Bring forth the roy-al di-a-dem, And crown him Lord of all;
To him all maj-es-ty as-cribe, And crown him Lord of all;
We'll join the ev-er-last-ing song, And crown him Lord of all;

Bring forth the roy-al di-a-dem, And crown him Lord of all.
To him all maj-es-ty as-cribe, And crown him Lord of all.
We'll join the ev-er-last-ing song, And crown him Lord of all.

"LO, I AM WITH YOU ALWAY." Concluded.

No. 109. PRAYER OF GETHSEMANE.

W. T. Giffe.   W. T. G.

PRAYER OE GETHSEMANE. Concluded.

prayer in Geth-sem-a-ne; Beau-ti-ful prayer of Geth-sem-a-ne.
will," be it e'er my plea; Beau-ti-ful prayer of Geth-sem-a-ne.
prayer of Geth-sem-a-ne; Beau-ti-ful prayer of Geth-sem-a-ne.

No. 110. THE LORD WILL PROVIDE.

Mrs. M. A. W. Cook.   W. G. Thomas.

1. In some way or oth-er The Lord will pro-vide;
2. At some time or oth-er The Lord will pro-vide;
3. De-spond then no long-er, The Lord will pro-vide;

It may not be my way, It may not be thy way;
It may not be my time, It may not be thy time;
And this be the to-ken, No word he hath spo-ken

And yet in his own way The Lord will pro-vide.
And yet in his own time The Lord will pro-vide.
Hath ev-er been bro-ken— The Lord will pro-vide.

No. 111. THE CITY OF GOLD.

MILO W. NETHERCUTT.

1. There's a cit-y that looks o'er the val-ley of death, And its glo-ries can nev-er be told; There the sun nev-er sets, and the leaves nev-er fade, In that beau-ti-ful cit-y of Gold.
2. There the King, our Re-deem-er, the Lord whom we love, All the faith-ful with rapt-ure be-hold; There the right-eous for-ev-er shall shine as the stars, In that beau-ti-ful cit-y of Gold.
3. Ev-'ry soul we have led to the foot of the cross, Ev-'ry lamb we have brought to the fold, Shall be kept as bright jew-els our crown to a-dorn, In that beau-ti-ful cit-y of Gold.

CHORUS.

There the sun nev-er sets, and the leaves nev-er fade, There the

GLIDING AWAY. Concluded.

No. 114.   WEBB.

For Music see No. 151.

1 Stand up, stand up for Jesus,
   Ye soldiers of the cross;
Lift high his royal banner,
   It must not suffer loss;
From victory unto victory
   His army shall he lead,
Till every foe is vanquished,
   And Christ is Lord indeed.

2 Stand up, stand up for Jesus,
   Stand in his strength alone;
The arm of flesh will fail you,
   Ye dare not trust your own;
Put on the gospel armor,
   Each piece put on with prayer;
Where duty calls, or danger,
   Be never wanting there.

3 Stand up, stand up for Jesus,
   The strife will not be long;
This day the noise of battle,
   The next the victor's song.
To him that overcometh,
   A crown of life shall be;
He with the King of glory
   Shall reign eternally.

No. 115. IT IS I, BE NOT AFRAID.

S. L. Cuthbert.   Jas. L. Orr.

1. When the mist-y clouds a-round you Hide the sunlight from your eyes,
2. Darkness here, yet still a-bove you Shines the gold-en cit-y bright;
3. With his presence ev-er near you, Needed aid and hope to bring,

And the darkness that surrounds you Veils the brightness of the skies;
On its streets are those who love you, Hap-py in its ra-diant light.
How his words should al-ways cheer you, Make your heart with joy to sing.

Then, when-e'er your cour-age fal-ters, Hear the words the Mas-ter said,
With your Sav-ior close be-side you, Do not fear, be not dismayed,
Oh, the light of day is shin-ing Far be-yond the clouds and shade,

When he walked up-on the wa-ters—It is I, be not a-fraid.
With his hand and voice to guide you—It is I, be not a-fraid.
No more dark-ness or re-pin-ing—It is I, be not a-fraid.

By permission.

IT IS I, BE NOT AFRAID. Concluded.

No. 116. THE SWEETEST NAME.

J. C. BRIDGE.

THE SWEETEST NAME. Concluded.

No. 117. JESUS IS THE WAY.

E. R. Latta. W. T. Giffe.

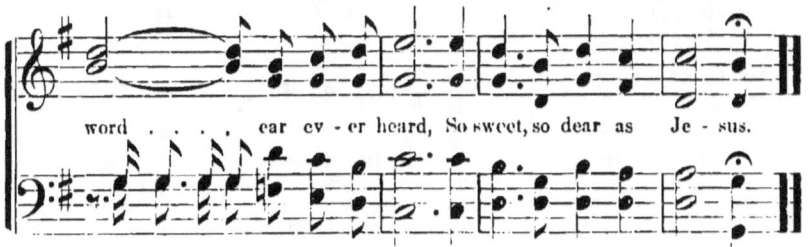

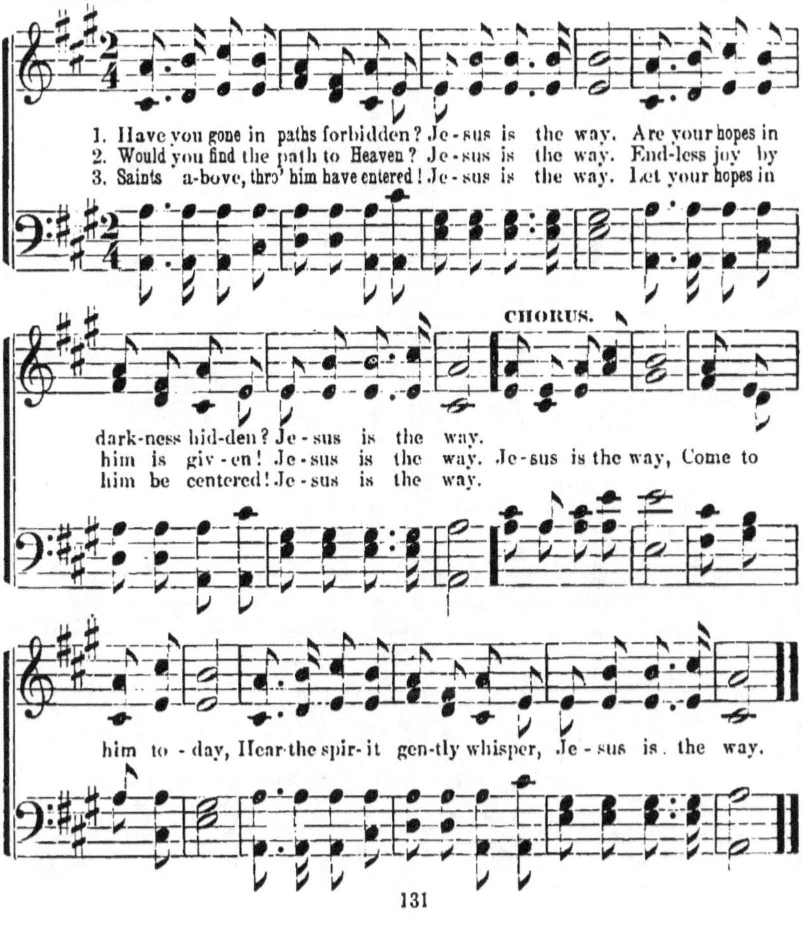

No. 118. BID THEM AHOY!

E. R. LATTA. W. T. GIFFE.

Earnestly.

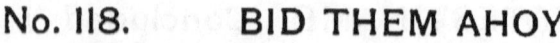

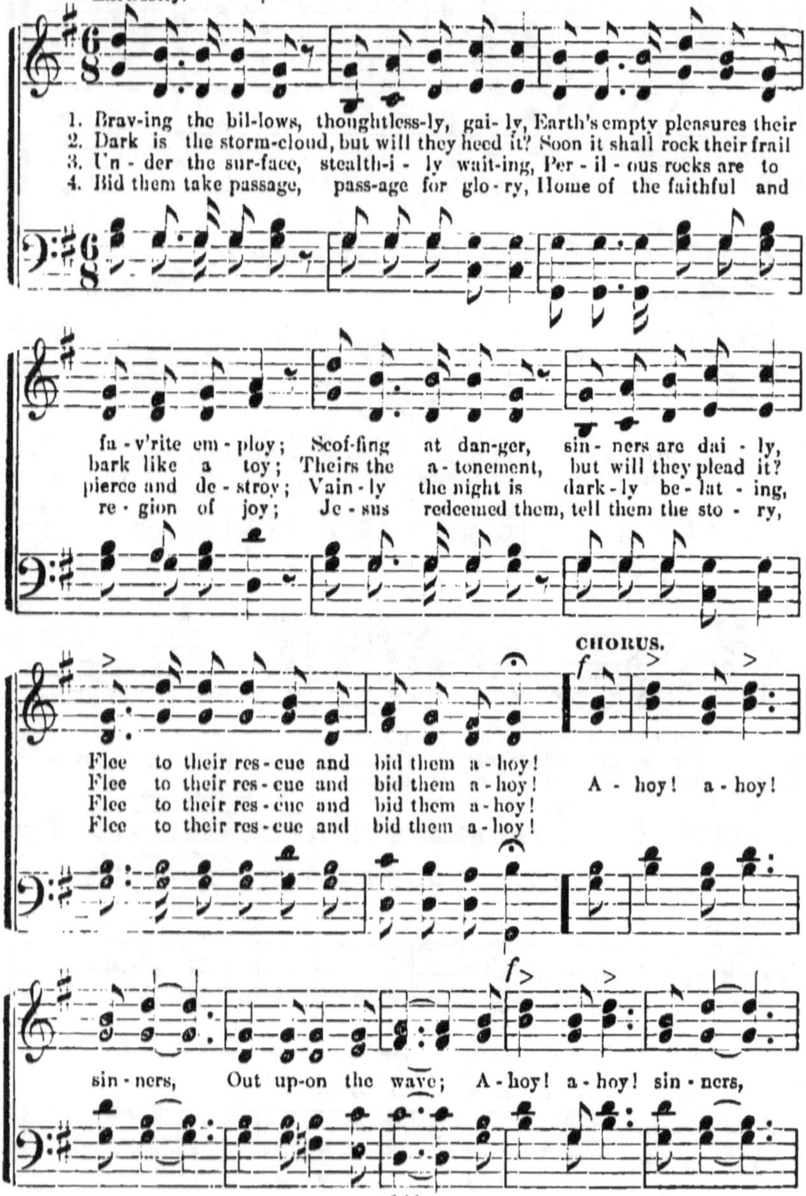

BID THEM AHOY! Concluded.

No. 119. MY SOUL, BE ON THY GUARD.

L. MASON.

REJOICE, YE RANSOMED. Concluded.

Press on-ward to the prize in view, For all who to the end are true.

No. 121. COME, THOU ALMIGHTY KING.

C. WESLEY.   (Italian Hymn, 6s. 4s.)   FELICE GIARDINI.

1. Come, thou al-might-y King, Help us thy name to sing,
2. Come, thou in-car-nate word, Gird on thy might-y sword,
3. Come, ho-ly Com-fort-er, Thy sa-cred wit-ness bear,

Help us to praise. Fa-ther all-glo-ri-ous, O'er all vic-
Our prayer at-tend; Come and thy peo-ple bless, And give thy
In this glad hour; Thou who al-might-y art, Now rule in

to-ri-ous, Come and reign o-ver us, An-cient of days.
word suc-cess; Spir-it of ho-li-ness, On us de-scend.
ev-'ry heart, And ne'er from us de-part, Spir-it of pow'r.

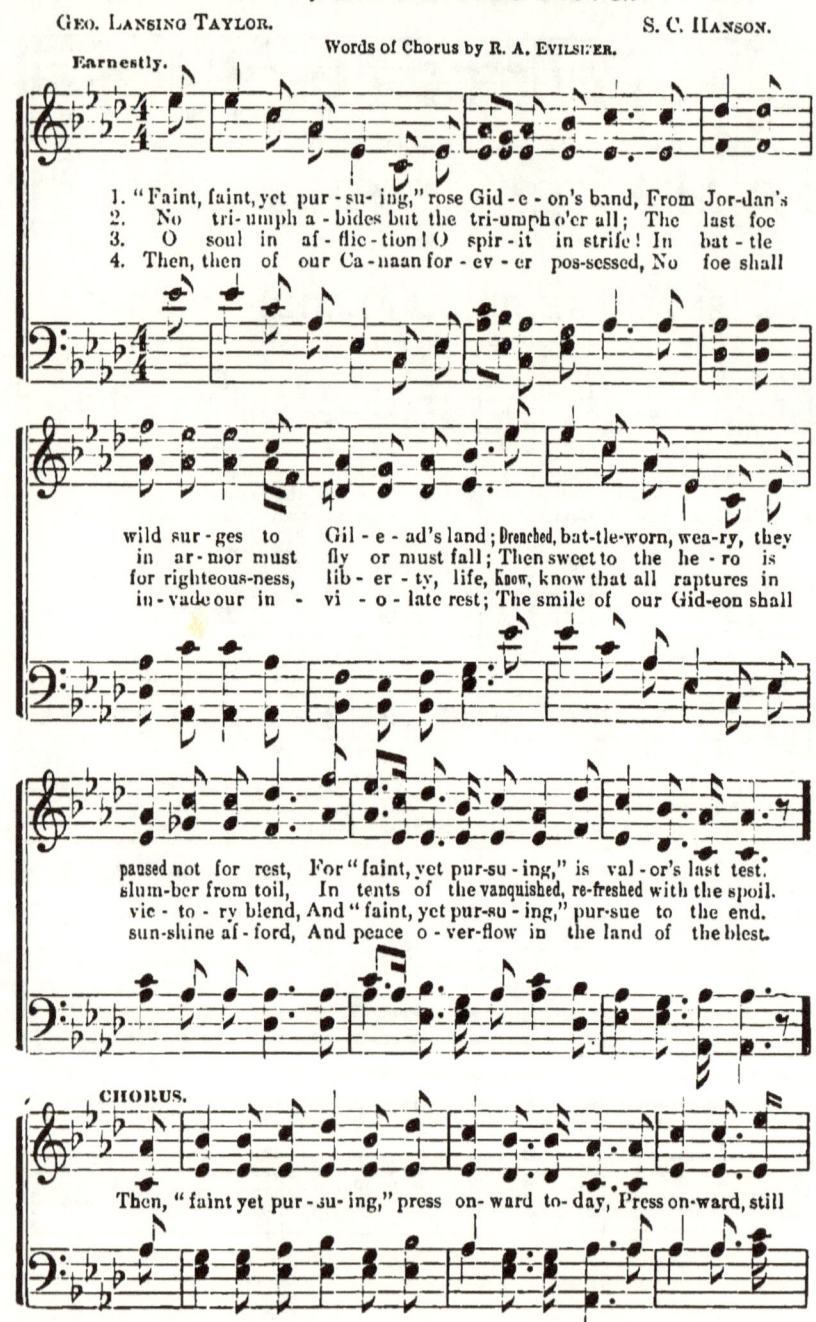

FAINT, YET PURSUING. Concluded.

on-ward and make no de-lay, God's ban-ner floats o'er us, our Gid-e-on leads, Strike bold-ly for heav-en with val-or-ous deeds.

No. 123. I'M A PILGRIM.

Mrs. Mary S. B. Dana.   German Melody.

1. I'm a pil-grim, and I'm a stran-ger, I can tar-ry, I can tar-ry but a night;
2. There, the glo-ry is ev-er shin-ing; Oh, my longing heart, my longing heart is there;
3. There's the cit-y to which I jour-ney; My Re-deemer, my Redeemer is its light;

Do not de-tain me, for I am go - ing To where the fountains are ev-er flow - ing.
Here in this country so dark and drear-y, I long have wandered for-lorn and wea - ry.
There is no sorrow, nor a-ny sigh - ing, Nor a-ny tears there, nor a-ny dy - ing.

BLUE SEA OF GALILEE. Concluded.

O calm blue sea! O sil-v'ry sea! Where our Redeemer loved to be;

O wondrous sea of Gal-i-lee! I love to think and dream of thee.

No. 125. RETREAT. L. M.

Dr. Thos. Hastings.

1. From ev-ery stormy wind that blows, From every swelling tide of woes,
2. There is a place where Je-sus sheds The oil of gladness on our heads—
3. There is a scene where spirits blend, Where friend holds fellowship with friend;

There is a calm, a sure re-treat; 'Tis found beneath the mer-cy-seat.
A place than all be-sides more sweet; It is the blood-bought mer-cy-seat.
Though sundered far, by faith they meet A-round one common mer-cy-seat.

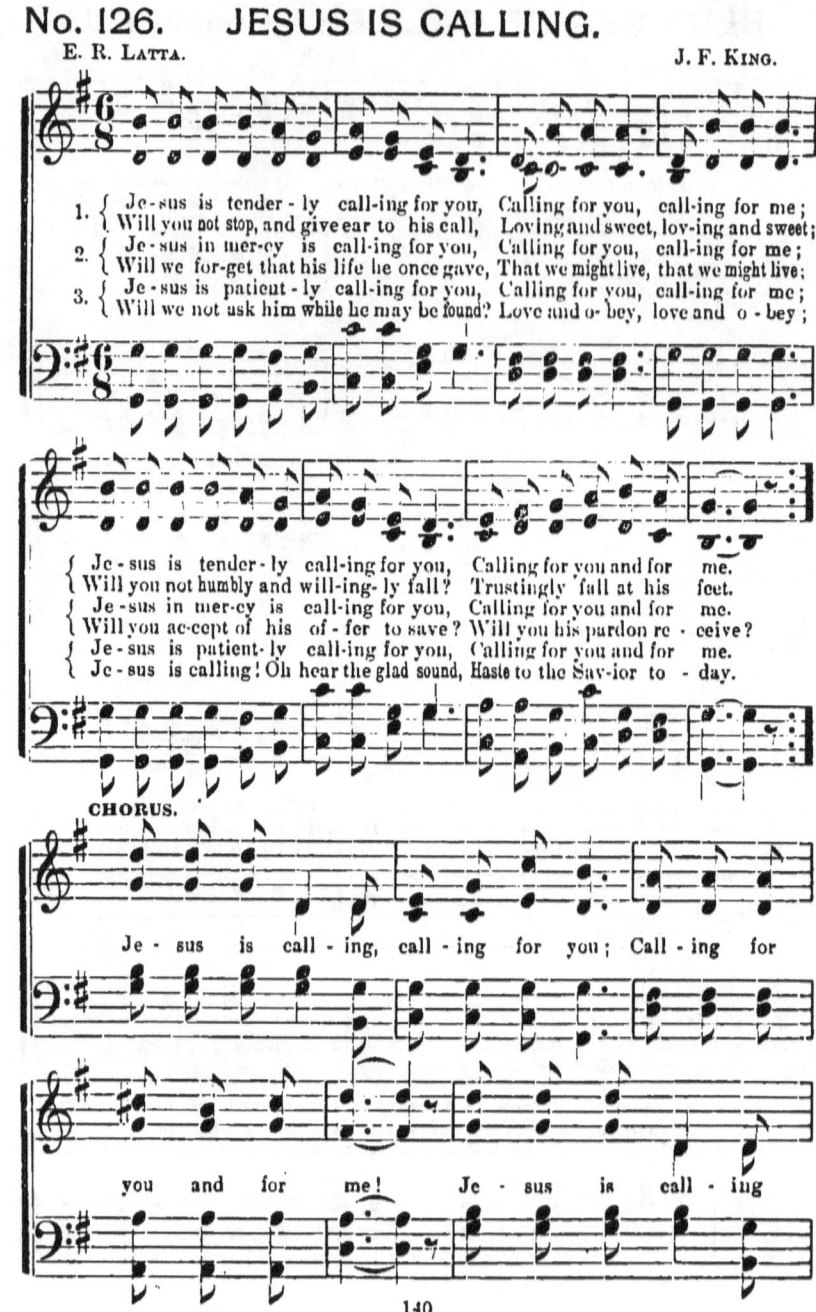

JESUS IS CALLING. Concluded.

call - ing for you, Call - ing for you and for me!

No. 127.   **AMERICA.**

Words by S. F. Smith.

Maestoso.

1. My coun - try, 'tis of thee, Sweet land of lib - er - ty,
2. My na - tive coun - try! thee, Land of the no - ble free,
3. Let mu - sic swell the breeze, And ring from all the trees
4. Our fa - ther's God, to thee, Au - thor of lib - er - ty,

Of thee I sing; Land where my fa - thers died, Land of the
Thy name I love; I love thy rocks and rills, Thy woods and
Sweet free - dom's song; Let mor - tal tongues a - wake, Let all that
To thee we sing; Long may our land be bright With freedom's

pilgrim's pride, From ev - 'ry mountain side, Let free - dom ring.
templed hills; My heart with rap-ture thrills, Like that a - bove.
breathe par-take, Let rocks their si - lence break, The sound pro - long.
ho - ly light; Pro - tect us by thy might, Great God our King.

No. 128. BRINGING THEM IN.

Arr. by E. N. C.
Not too fast.
Dr. E. N. Campbell.

1. To our dear Sabbath-school there ought many to come, Who spend Sunday wand'ring or trifling at home; I'll try to bring *one*, or I'll try to bring *two*, Yes, all that I can I'm determined to do. God meant all the people who live in this place To hear of his
2. Let me think: are there none of the dear ones at home, The large or the little, who never have come? Oh, I'll beg and I'll coax, try for *one*, try for *two*, Yes, all that I can I'm determined to do. My neighbors and playmates who live on my street, I'll ask them to
3. How many there be whom I pass every day, Who spend all their Sundays in frolic and play; If I could get *one* of them now, or get *two*, To come here next Sabbath, what good it might do. I hope that to heaven some day I will go, What glory and

BRINGING THEM IN. Continued.

143

BRINGING THEM IN. Concluded.

try to bring *two,* Yes, all that I can I'm de-termined to do.

No. 129. "I'M KNEELING AT THE DOOR."

LYDIA C. BAXTER.   HENRY A. LEWIS.

1. I'm kneeling, Lord, at mer-cy's gate, With trembling hope and fear;
2. None ev-er emp-ty turned a-way Who 'tru-ly sought thy face;

I've wait-ed long, and still I wait, Thy gra-cious word to hear;
And I, my Sav-ior, come to-day, To seek thy pard'ning grace;

Thy precious word has bid me seek The joys thou hast in store;
Thy precious blood is all my plea, This can my soul re-store;

Copyright, 1892, by HENRY A. LEWIS.

"I'M KNEELING." Concluded.

OUR HAPPY HOME BEYOND. Concluded.

No. 131. SWEET HOUR OF PRAYER.

1 Sweet hour of prayer, sweet hour of prayer,
That calls me from a world of care,
And bids me, at my Father's throne,
Make all my wants and wishes known.
In seasons of distress and grief,
My soul has often found relief,
And oft escaped the tempter's snare,
By thy return, sweet hour of prayer.

2 Sweet hour of prayer, sweet hour of prayer
Thy wings shall my petition bear
To him whose truth and faithfulness
Engage the waiting soul to bless;
And since he bids me seek his face,
Believe his word and trust his grace,
I'll cast on him my every care,
And wait for thee, sweet hour of prayer.

A WORD FOR JESUS. Concluded.

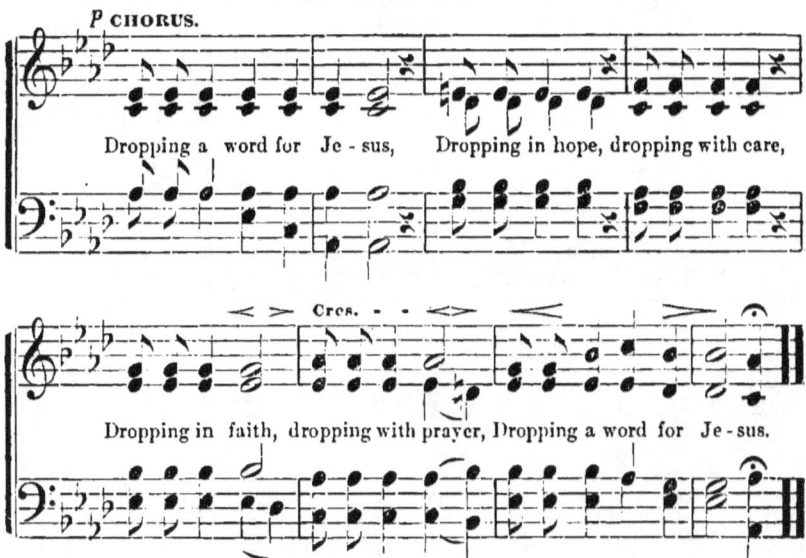

No. 133. HOW SWEET, HOW HEAVENLY.

Wm. B. Bradbury.

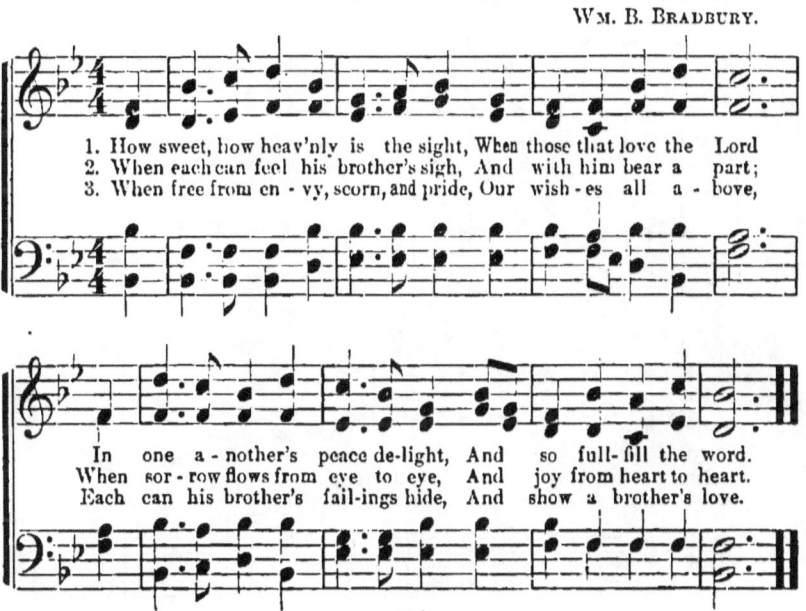

No. 134. CHRIST IS RISEN.

M. M. B. (Easter.) Mrs. Mary M. Bowen.

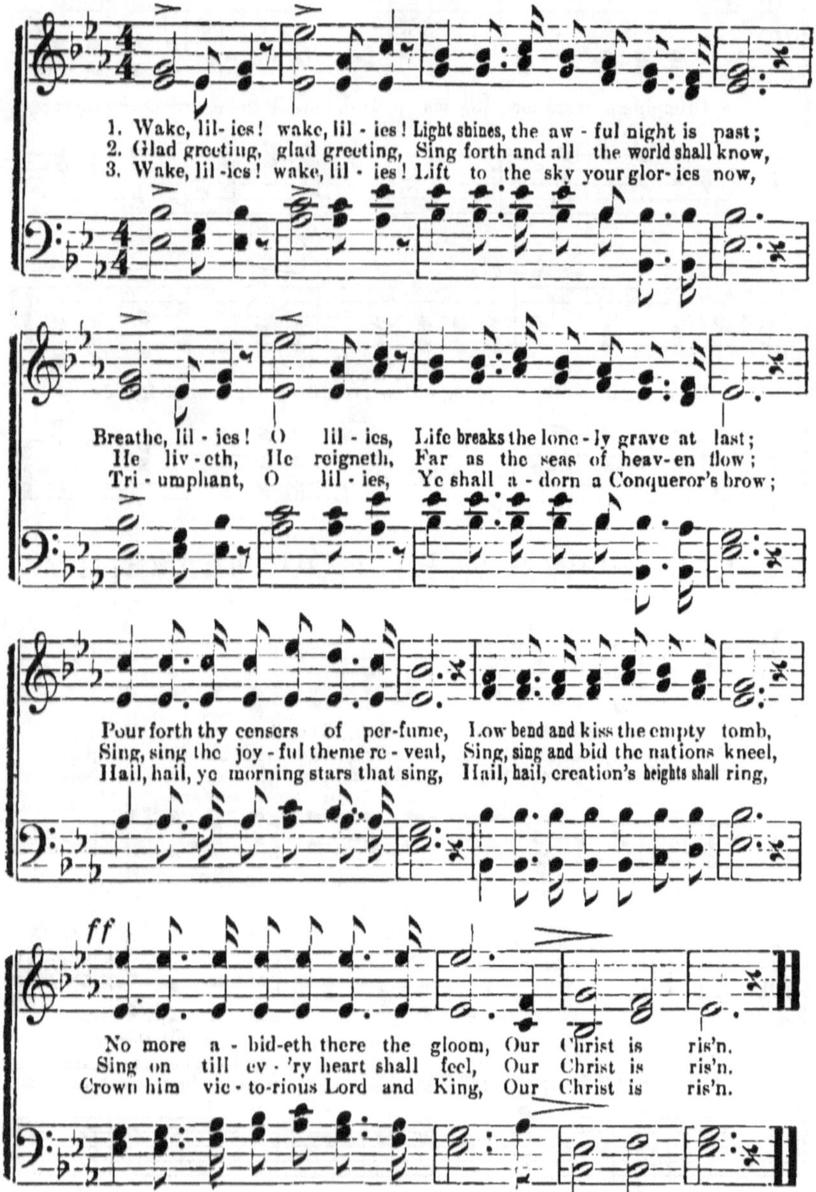

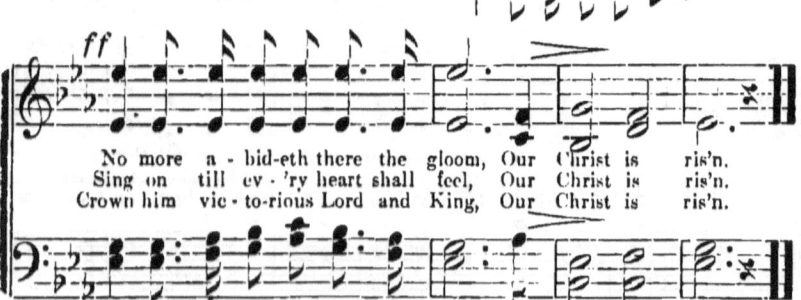

SOMEWHERE. Concluded.

No. 137. HO! REAPERS.
Tune—Webb.

1 Ho! reapers of life's harvest,
　Why stand with rusted blade,
Until the night draws round thee,
　And day begins to fade?
Why stand ye idle, waiting
　For reapers more to come?
The golden morn is passing,
　Why sit ye idle, dumb?

2 Mount up the heights of wisdom,
　And crush each error low,
Keep back no words of knowledge
　That human hearts should know.
Be faithful to thy mission,
　In service of the Lord,
And in the golden harvest
　Shall be thy great reward.

No. 139. ON THE HUSKS.

E. R. LATTA.   W. T. GIFFE.

1. On the husks are you feeding, my brother, With none for you to care?
2. Do you feel you are wretched, my brother, And ev-er-more un-done?
3. If your heart is re-pent-ant, my brother, You need not be a-fraid!

In the house of your Fa-ther, my brother, There's plen-ty, and to spare.
Would you be as a serv-ant, my brother, And not your Father's son?
As a son you'll be reckoned, my brother, A feast for you be made.

CHORUS.

He, a-far, will be-hold you, And tender-ly, tender-ly will call!

He will come out to meet you, And on your neck will fall.

I NEED THEE, LORD. Concluded.

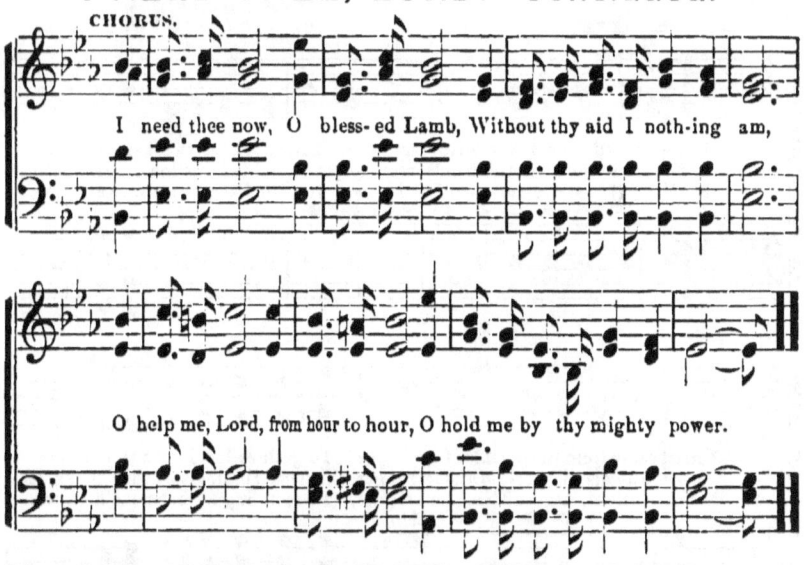

No. 143. JESUS, LOVER OF MY SOUL.
C. WESLEY. (MARTYN. 7s. DOUBLE.) S. B. MARSH.

2 Other refuge have I none,
  Hangs my helpless soul on thee;
  Leave, O leave me not alone!
  Still support and comfort me;
  All my trust on thee is stayed,
  All my help from thee I bring;
  Cover my defenseless head
  With the shadow of thy wing.

3 Thou, O Christ, art all I want,
  More than all in thee I find;
  Raise the fallen, cheer the faint,
  Heal the sick, and lead the blind.
  Just and holy is thy name,
  I am all unrighteousness;
  False and full of sin I am,
  Thou art full of truth and grace.

O, TELL THE SWEET STORY! Concluded.

No. 145. GOD OF THE NATIONS.
(PATRIOTIC.) German.

1. Great God of na-tions, now to thee Our hymn of grat-i-tude we raise;
2. Here freedom spreads her banner wide, And casts her soft and hallowed ray;
3. Great God, preserve us in thy fear, In danger still our guard-ian be;

With humble heart and bending knee, We of-fer thee our song of praise.
Here thou our fathers' steps didst guide In safety thro' their dangerous way.
O spread thy truth's bright precepts here, Let all the peo - ple wor-ship thee.

WOULD YOU KNOW? Concluded.

his love en-treat-ing, Will you go? will you go?
love en-treat - ing, Will you go? ... will you go?

No. 147.   NEARER THE CROSS.

FRANK M. DAVIS.   "The Cross of our Lord Jesus Christ."—Gal. 6: 14.   J. H. HALL.

1. Near-er the cross of Je - sus, Ev - er let me be;
2. Near-er the cross of Je - sus, There I would a - bide;
3. Near-er the cross of Je - sus, Let me live and die;

Near - er the flow - ing fount - ain, That cleans-eth me.
There let me rest for - ev - er, Near Je - sus' side.
There I will find sweet ref - uge, And safe - ty nigh.

D. S. Near-er the flow - ing foun - tain, That cleans - eth me.

CHORUS.

Near-er the cross, Near-er the cross, Near-er the cross of Je - sus.

TURN, TURN TO HIM. Concluded.

TELL IT OUT! Concluded.

WHY NOT TO-NIGHT. Concluded.

CHORUS. Earnestly.

Why not to-night? why not to-night? Thou would'st be saved, why not to-night?
why not to-night? why not to-night?

Rit.

Why not to-night? why not to-night? Thou would'st be saved, why not to-night?
to-night?

No. 151. WEBB.

For Words see No. 114.

GEORGE JAMES WEBB.

THE SEED OF THE WORD. Concluded.

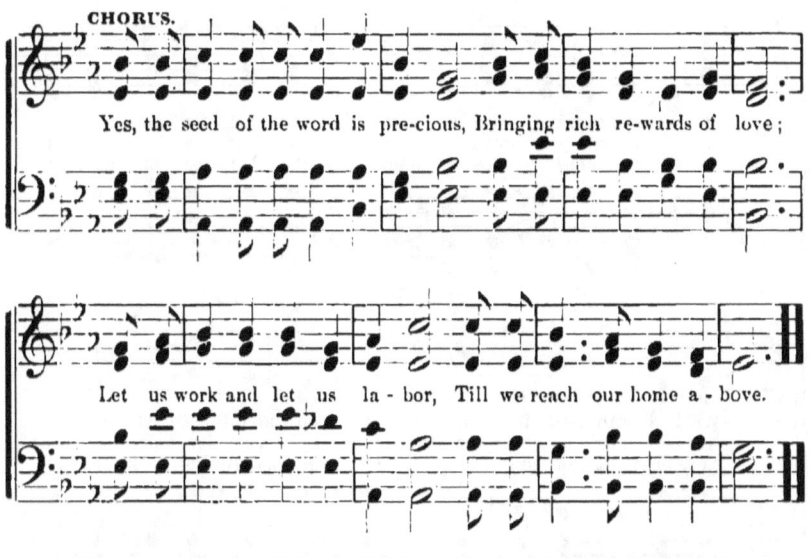

No. 153. HOW SWEET AND HEAVENLY.

DEODATUS DUTTON, Jr.

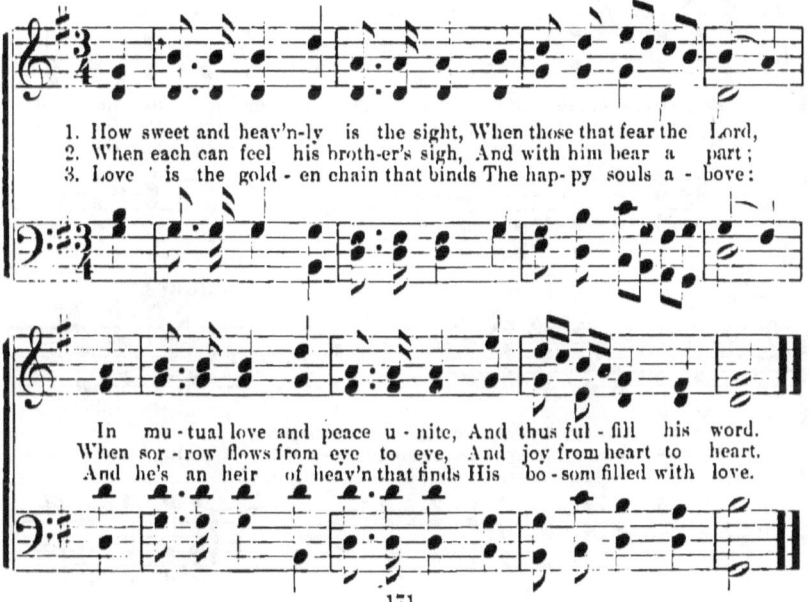

1. How sweet and heav'nly is the sight, When those that fear the Lord, In mu-tual love and peace u-nite, And thus ful-fill his word.
2. When each can feel his broth-er's sigh, And with him bear a part; When sor-row flows from eye to eye, And joy from heart to heart.
3. Love is the gold-en chain that binds The hap-py souls a-bove; And he's an heir of heav'n that finds His bo-som filled with love.

WE ARE COMING HOME. Concluded.

Coming home to-night, Bless-ed Sav-iour, we by faith re-ceive our sight, (receive our sight,) We are com-ing, bless-ed Je-sus, Com-ing at thy call, We are com-ing, we are coming home to-night.

No. 155. NOW BE THE GOSPEL BANNER.

Tune—WEBB, No. 151.

1 Now be the Gospel banner
   In every land unfurled,
 And be the shout "Hosanna!"
   Re-echoed through the world:
 Till every isle and nation,
   Till every tribe and tongue,
 Receive the great salvation,
   And join the happy throng.

2 What though th' embattled legions
   Of earth and hell combine?
 His power throughout their regions,
   Shall soon resplendent shine;
 Ride on, O Lord, victorious,
   Immanuel, prince of peace;
 Thy triumph shall be glorious,
   Thine empire still increase.

3 Yes, thou shalt reign forever,
   O Jesus, King of kings:
 Thy light, thy love, thy favor,
   Each ransomed captive sings.
 The isles for thee are waiting,
   The deserts learn thy praise,
 The hills and valleys greeting,
   The song responsive raise.

IF YOU WILL. Concluded.

will, You may know Christ's saving power, If you will,
if you will, if you will.

No. 157. I CAN NOT DRIFT BEYOND.

LAURA E. NEWELL. W. T. GIFFE.

1. I can not drift be-yond his love, Or past his care or sight;
2. I can not drift be-yond his love, If days be bright or dim;
3. I can not drift be-yond his care, If those I love the best
4. I can not drift be-yond his love, No last-ing grief is mine,

And if life's way leads thro' grief's maze, Or flood-ed is with light,
For lo! my hand is clasped in his, And I shall fol-low him;
Close their dear eyes, no more to wake, And I am grief op-pressed;
For he whose promise can not fail— E-ter-nal and di-vine—

I can not drift beyond his love, Who guards and guides me from above.
Tho' madly tossed on life's rough sea, Yet 'tis my Pi-lot guid-ing me.
It is his hand that dries my tears, And gently leads me down the years.
Is hold-ing me, I shall not fall, He is my strength, my life, my all.

LET ME DWELL. Concluded.

near thy side, ... In thy love . . may I a-bide. . . . . .
er, . . ev-er near thy side, . . In thy love, thy love may I a-bide.

Bless-ed Sav-ior, bless-ed Sav-ior, In thy pres-ence I would e'er a-bide.

No. 159. BETHANY.

1 Nearer, my God, to thee,
　Nearer to thee!
　E'en though it be a cross
　　That raiseth me;
　Still all my song shall be,
　Nearer, my God, to thee,
　　Nearer to thee!

2 Though like the wanderer
　　The sun gone down,
　Darkness be over me,
　　My rest a stone;
　Yet in my dreams I'd be
　Nearer, my God, to thee,
　　Nearer to thee.

3 There let the way appear
　　Steps unto heaven;
　All that thou send'st to me,
　　In mercy given;

Angels to beckon me
Nearer, my God, to thee,
　Nearer to thee.

4 Then with my waking thoughts
　　Bright with thy praise,
　Out of my stony griefs
　　Bethel I'll raise;
　So by my woes to be
　Nearer, my God to thee,
　　Nearer to thee.

5 Or if on joyful wing
　　Cleaving the sky,
　Sun, moon, and stars forgot,
　　Upwards I fly,
　Still all my song shall be,
　Nearer, my God, to thee,
　　Nearer to thee.

NEARER EVERY DAY. Concluded.

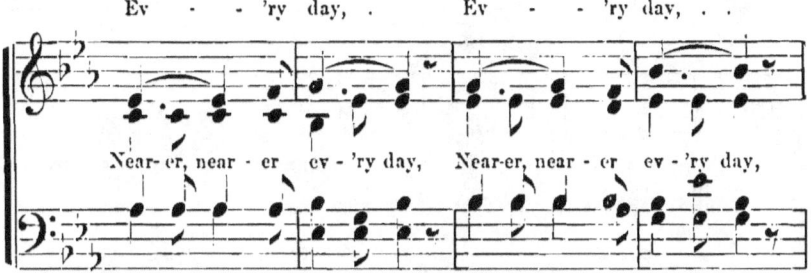

No. 163. THE MORNING LIGHT.
TUNE; WEBB, No. 151.

1 The morning light is breaking,
　The darkness disappears;
　The sons of earth are waking
　　To penitential tears;
　Each breeze that sweeps the ocean
　　Brings tidings from afar,
　Of nations in commotion,
　　Prepared for Zion's war.

2 Blest river of salvation,
　　Pursue thine onward way;
　Flow thou to every nation,
　　Nor in thy richness stay.
　Stay not till all the lowly
　　Triumphant reach their home;
　Stay not till all the holy
　　Proclaim, "The Lord is come!"

No. 165. COURAGE, PILGRIM.

Mrs. Harriet E. Jones.   Frank M. Davis.

1. Are you toil-ing day by day, Thro' a dark and storm-y way?
2. Have you bur-ied all your own, Do you journey all a-lone?
3. With your eyes up-on the cross, Bear with meekness pain and loss;

Cour-age, pil-grim! rest a - waits Just be-yond the pear-ly gates.
Cour-age, pil-grim! some glad time, Blest re-un-ion in yon clime.
By and by a grand re-ward, In the Kingdom of our Lord.

CHORUS.

Press on, pil-grim, fal-ter nev-er, Just be-yond the sil-ent riv-er,

rit. ad lib.

In the bright, the glad for-ev-er, Rest and joy a-waits for thee.

SEND OUT THE LIFE-BOAT. Concluded.

toss-ing in a frail bark; The news of sal-va-tion, oh, take it to him, And Je-sus will help you his soul to win.

No. 167. AM I A SOLDIER?

Isaac Watts.   Thos. A. Arne.

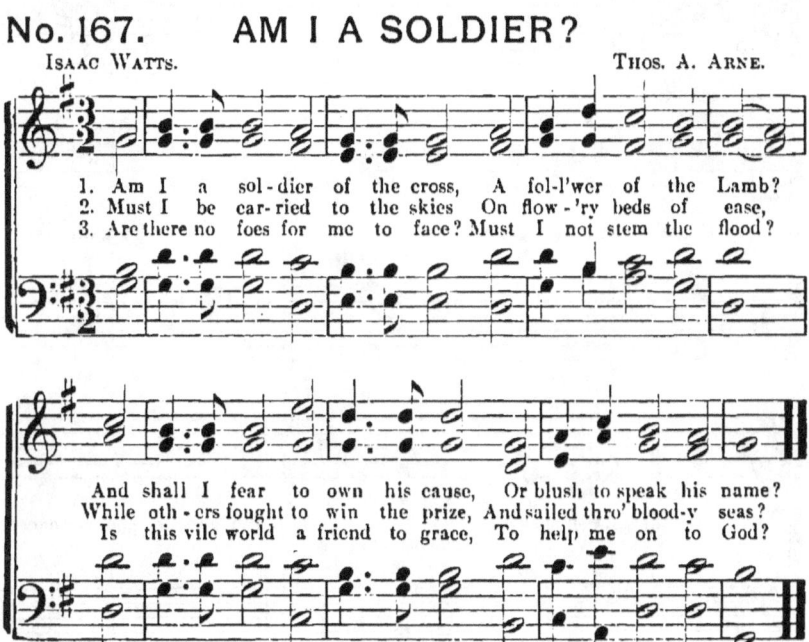

1. Am I a sol-dier of the cross, A fol-l'wer of the Lamb?
2. Must I be car-ried to the skies On flow-'ry beds of ease,
3. Are there no foes for me to face? Must I not stem the flood?

And shall I fear to own his cause, Or blush to speak his name?
While oth-ers fought to win the prize, And sailed thro' blood-y seas?
Is this vile world a friend to grace, To help me on to God?

WHEN THE ANGEL REAPERS. Concluded.

well, Or noth - ing bring but worthless leaves?
yes, be ladened well. worthless leaves.

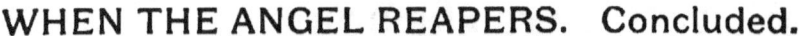

No. 169. TRUSTING IN THY PROMISE.

IDA L. REED. FRANK M. DAVIS.

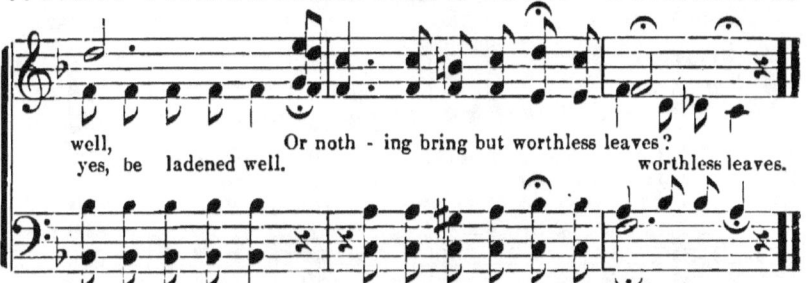

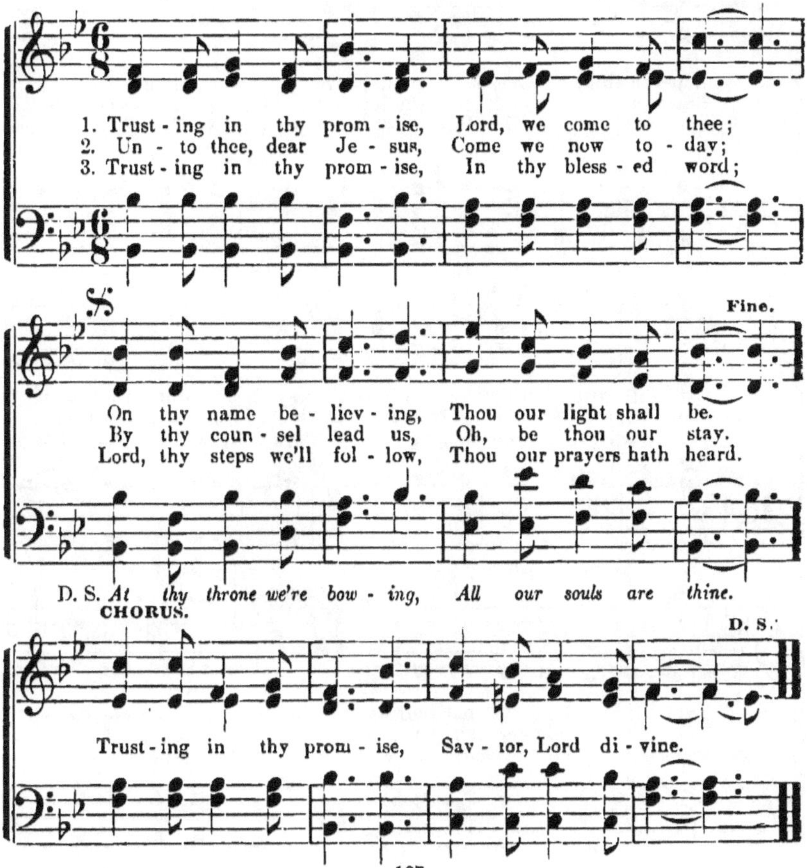

1. Trust - ing in thy prom - ise, Lord, we come to thee;
2. Un - to thee, dear Je - sus, Come we now to - day;
3. Trust - ing in thy prom - ise, In thy bless - ed word;
Fine.
On thy name be - liev - ing, Thou our light shall be.
By thy coun - sel lead us, Oh, be thou our stay.
Lord, thy steps we'll fol - low, Thou our prayers hath heard.
D. S. At thy throne we're bow - ing, All our souls are thine.
CHORUS.
D. S.
Trust - ing in thy prom - ise, Sav - ior, Lord di - vine.

DAYS ARE GOING BY. Concluded.

No. 171. OH, FOR A HEART TO PRAISE.

Rev. Chas. Wesley.

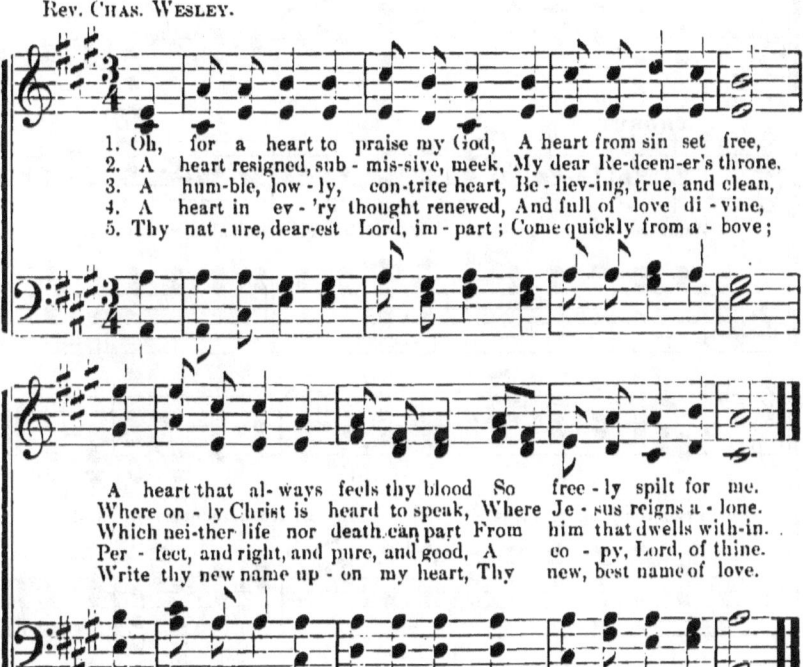

No. 172. STEP OVER THE LINE.

Ida L. Reed. Frank M. Davis.

1. Step o-ver the line, my broth-er, Come out on the Sav-ior's side;
2. Step o-ver the line, my broth-er, The shadows are deep'ning round;
3. Step o-ver the line, my broth-er, To Je-sus yield all thy soul;

Choose him far a-bove a-ny oth-er, Your friend and your dai-ly guide.
De-lay not, he waits for thy com-ing, Step o-ver on ho-ly ground.
Come in-to his love's sweetest sun-light, Let him all thy ways con-trol.

CHORUS.

Step o-ver the line, my broth-er, Wait not till an-oth-er day;
Choose Je-sus to be for-ev-er The staff of your pil-grim way.

No. 174. MY TRUST ON THEE IS STAYED.

LAURA E. NEWELL.   HUBERT P. MAIN.

1. My trust is stayed on thee, O Lord, My hope in thee a-lone;
2. My trust on thee is ev-er stayed, Blest Savior, tried and dear;
3. When paths are rough and dark and wild, And tempest-tost I stray,

Thro' weal or woe thou art my friend, The dear-est ev-er known.
Thy child shall nev-er be dis-mayed, For now the skies are clear.
I call up-on thy gra-cious name To guide me in thy way.

No foes by night or day may harm, My soul shall feel no fear;
Lord, at thy feet I low-ly kneel, And ask thy bless-ing there;
Then lead me by thy lov-ing hand, As thro' earth's wilds I roam;

My trust on thee is stayed, O Lord, And thou art ev-er near.
O Fa-ther, be thy love revealed, And keep me in thy care.
Make me and keep me thine a-lone, Till thou shalt call me home.

Copyright, 1892, by HUBERT P. MAIN.

No. 179. WHITER THAN THE SNOW.

GEORGE D. BUCHANAN.

1. Come, my Redeemer, come, And deign to dwell with me;
Come, and thy right assume, And bid thy rivals flee—
2. Exert thy mighty power And banish all my sin;
In this auspicious hour, Bring all thy graces in—
3. Rule thou in every thought And passion of my soul,
Till all my powers are brought Beneath thy full control—

REFRAIN.
Come, my Redeemer, quickly come,
Come, my Redeemer, quickly come, And make my heart thy lasting home,
Come, my Redeemer, come,
Wash me in the blood of the

By permission.

WHITER THAN THE SNOW. Concluded.

DRIFTING, LORD, TO THEE. Concluded.

No. 181. IN WHOM I HAVE REDEMPTION.

F. M. D.
Frank M. Davis.

1. I know in whom I have re-demp-tion, In whom I have be-lieved; Whence cometh peace that pass-eth knowledge, That sav-ing grace re-ceived.
2. I know that he who stilled the tem-pest Has touched my trou-bled heart; Re-newed within my fainting spir-it, And bade my fears de-part.
3. I know that some day I shall see him In yon bright courts a-bove, And bear the likeness of my Sav-ior— Saved by re-deem-ing love.

CHORUS.

'Tis noth-ing that . . . . . . I've done to mer-it This love that Christ . . . . . . for me has shown; . . . . . . He sought me

'Tis nothing that I've done to merit This love that Christ for me has shown;

IN WHOM I'VE REDEMPTION. Concluded.

No. 182.   SONGS OF PRAISE.

W. S. Montgomery.

1. Songs of praise the an - gels sang, Heav'n with hal - le - lu - jahs rang,
2. Songs of praise a - woke the morn When the Prince of Peace was born;
3. Heav'n and earth must pass a - way, Songs of praise shall crown that day;

When Je - hov-ah's work be - gun, When he spake and it was done.
Songs of praise a - rose when he Cap - tive led cap - tiv - i - ty.
God will make new heav'n and earth, Songs of praise shall hail their birth.

No. 185. FAR FROM HOME.

LAURA E. NEWELL. FRANK M. DAVIS.

FAR FROM HOME. Concluded.

"Fear not, I'll res-cue thee, I came to save the lost."

No. 186. TELL JESUS.

GEORGIANA M. TAYLOR.   MILO W. NETHERCUTT.

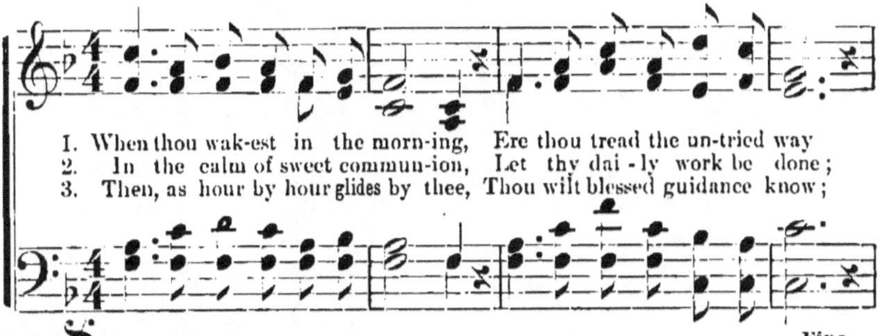

1. When thou wak-est in the morn-ing, Ere thou tread the un-tried way
2. In the calm of sweet commun-ion, Let thy dai-ly work be done;
3. Then, as hour by hour glides by thee, Thou wilt blessed guidance know;

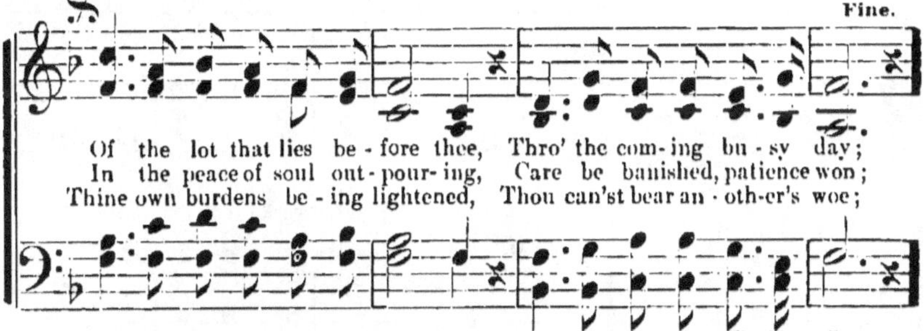

Of the lot that lies be-fore thee, Thro' the com-ing bu-sy day;
In the peace of soul out-pour-ing, Care be banished, patience won;
Thine own burdens be-ing lightened, Thou can'st bear an-oth-er's woe;

D. S. *Be thy dawn-ing glad or gloom-y,* Go to Je-sus—tell him all!
D. S. *Ere thou list-en—ere thou an-swer,* Turn to Je-sus—tell him all!
D. S. *But re-mem-ber, while thou serv-est,* Still tell Je-sus—tell him all!

Whether sunbeams promise bright-ness, Whether dim fore-bod-ings fall,
And if earth with its en-chant-ments Seek thy spir-it to en-thrall,
Thou can'st help the weak ones on-ward, Thou can'st raise up those that fall;

No. 188. INTO THE FOLD.

LAURA E. NEWELL.   FRANK M. DAVIS.

1. Now the good Shepherd is call-ing his sheep In-to the fold,
2. See, now, he car-ries the lambs on his breast In-to the fold,
3. Ten-der-ly, sweet-ly he's call-ing to-day, In-to the fold,

in-to the fold; O-ver them all lov-ing watch he doth keep, Se-
in-to the fold; Safe in his bo-som the lit-tle ones rest, With
in-to the fold, All now who wan-der from him far a-way, In

CHORUS.

cure from the storm and the cold.
him they shall nev-er grow old.   In-to the fold, in-to the fold, Whose
danger throughout the dark wold.

joys are untold; Into the fold, into the fold, Safe in the good Shepherd's fold.

INDEX.

Titles in Small Capitals.   First Lines in Roman Letters.

	No.
As Thy Days Thy Strength	37
Abide With Me	42
Anywhere My Savior Leads	47
Anywhere the blessed Savior	47
As doves to their windows	65
At my work I'm always singing	103
All hail the power of Jesus	107
America	127
Are you dropping a word	132
As panting in the sultry beam	148
Am I a Soldier?	167
A Song of Faith	45
A Word for Jesus	132
Are you toiling day by day	165
Angel Reapers, The	168
Beyond the Blue	11
Bring Them In	16
Bring them in and keep	16
Blessed Savior lead us gently	23
Behold, I stand at the door	27
Beautiful Hills, The	29
By waters cool and sweet	40
Bring Beautiful Lilies	52
Beautiful Home Land	59
Blessed Jesus, Take my Hand	69
Beautiful Land, The	81
Beautiful lights along the shore	101
Bid Them Ahoy	118
Braving the billows	118
Bringing Them In	128
Bethany	159
Children for Jesus, The	2
Children of Heaven	50
Come, Little One	55
Christian Battle Song	62
Children's Praises	66
Come with all thy sorrow	94
Christian War Song	98
Coronation, C. M.	107
City of Gold, The	111
Come, Thou Almighty King	121
Christ is Risen	134
Christmas Message, The	135
Courage, Pilgrim	165
Come, my Redeemer, come	179
Christmas Morning	70
Darkness falls upon our pathway	9
Do Thy Little	28
Doves To Their Windows	65

	No.
Down at The Cross	160
Days Are Going By, The	170
Drifting, Lord, To Thee	180
Father, I scarcely dare to pray	26
Father, Take Me by The Hand	30
Find In Christ Your Rest	57
Father, we welcome this glad	68
Forward, The Master Calls	76
Far from Home	185
God's Eye Watches	3
Gushing Rill, The	13
God Is My Guide	19
God Holds The Key	36
Gospel Bells	5
God Bless My Boy	46
Great Physician of Jericho, The	51
God Bless The Little Ones	58
Gather The Lost Ones In	61
Gather The Grain	71
Go and labor in my vineyard	71
Gliding Away	113
God of The Nations	145
Great God of Nations	145
Go work to-day for your	187
He Leads Thee On	12
Hold Thou My Hand	25
He Stands at The Door	27
Have you touched the garments	31
He Will Guide Thee Home	38
He is waiting to-day	38
Heaven Enough for Me	43
Heav'n is gathering up	44
Happy Thoughts	53
How sweet and soothing	53
Heaven Is My Home	80
Have you gone in paths forbidden	117
How Sweet, How Heavenly	153
Ho! Reapers	137
How Sweet and Heavenly	133
Hail, Happy Day	14
Help Us to Watch and Pray	72
I'll Knock At Mercy's Door	7
I know that my Redeemer lives	45
I Have No Friend Like Jesus	49
I love to think of the children	50
I'm a Pilgrim Going Home	60
I am on my pilgrim journey	60
Is My Name Written There	63

(206)

INDEX.

	No.		No.
In the lamb's book of life	63	Mighty army of the young	73
I am but a little child	69	My hands are thine	74
If we only sought to brighten	78	MORNING OF LIFE	100
In the loving shepherd's care	79	MY SOUL, BE ON THY GUARD	119
I'm but a stranger here	80	My country 'tis of thee	127
I KNOW IT IS THERE	83	My voice thou shalt hear	140
I rejoice now to know	83	MAKE ME A GLEANER FOR THEE	161
I WOULD LIVE LIKE JESUS	90	MORNING LIGHT, The	163
I'm a sinner all undone	96	MY TRUST IS STAYED ON THEE	174
In the shadow of his wings	108		
In some way or other	110	NIGHT HYMN	9
IT IS I, BE NOT AFRAID	115	NOTHING FURTHER I NEED	67
I'M KNEELING AT THE DOOR	129	NOTHING LEFT UNDONE	86
I'm kneeling, Lord, at mercy's gate	129	NEARER HOME	91
In that glorious morning bright	136	NO NIGHT IN GLORY	106
I NEED THEE, LORD	142	NEARER THE CROSS	147
I've heard such a wonderful	144	Nearer, my God, to thee	159
If we only sought to lighten	78	NEARER EVERY DAY	162
IF YOU WILL	156	Nearer to probation's close	162
I CANNOT DRIFT BEYOND	157	NOW BE THE GOSPEL BANNER	155
I WANT TO BE WHOLE	164	Now the Good Shepherd	188
IN WHOM I HAVE REDEMPTION	181		
Into the fold	188	Oh, if for me the cup you fill	13
		Oh! the beautiful hills	29
JERICHO SERVICE, The	51	O Christian, awake	35
JESUS LIVES	73	Oh, how sweetly sound	39
Jesus is calling	100	OUR JEWELS	44
Jesus calls the little children	102	OLD TIMES	48
JESUS IS THE WAY	117	OUT OF CHRIST	56
JESUS IS CALLING	126	Once was heard the song of children	66
Jesus is tenderly calling	126	ONWARD MARCH	75
JESUS IS BORN TO-DAY	141	O little town of Bethlehem	77
JESUS, LOVER OF MY SOUL	143	One sweetly solemn thought	91
		Oh wonderful place where Jesus	109
KNOCKING AT THE DOOR	84	OLD HUNDRED	112
		O blessed day, O happy hour	120
LEAD US GENTLY	23	OUR HAPPY HOME BEYOND	130
LET YOUR LIGHT SHINE	33	ON THE HUSKS	139
LAST PRAYER, A	26	O, TELL THE SWEET STORY	144
LITTLE TOWN OF BETHLEHEM	77	Oh! do not let the word depart	150
Lord of Life, The	84	Oh! I think I see the Master	152
LISTENING FOR THE MASTER	88	Oh, fathomless fountain of mercy	164
LET ME CLING TO THY HAND	89	OH, FOR A HEART TO PRAISE	171
LOVING JESUS	99	Out from thy bountiful hand	72
LIGHTS ALONG THE SHORE, The	101		
LET US FORWARD MARCH	104	PRAYER OF GETHSEMANE	109
"LO, I AM WITH YOU ALWAYS"	108	Praise God, from whom	112
LORD WILL PROVIDE, The	110	Peace, peace on earth	135
LET ME DWELL	158		
Let your trust be Jesus' love	170	REVIVE THY WORK	1
Little Children, can you tell	70	ROCK OF AGES	17
		Ruined and wretched, I come	67
My sins are great and many	7	REMEMBER ME	105
MEMORY OF GALILEE	15	REJOICE, YE RANSOMED	120
My heart goes out to Galilee	15	RALLYING SONG	175
MESSIAH IS COME	21		
MY SHEPHERD LEADS	40	SINGING SONGS FOR JESUS	8
Many are the homes that are dark	54	STANDING BY THE CROSS	10

INDEX.

Title	No.
Sweet the moments rich in blessing	10
Speak to Me, My Savior	18
Speak low to me, my Savior dear	18
Secret Prayer	22
Sweetest hours this side of heav'n	22
Some Sweet Day	34
Stand Like The Brave	35
Salvation Bells	39
Song of Faith, A	45
Send a shout along the line	62
Sabbath Song	68
Safe in the Fold	79
Speak Loving Words	87
Singing All The Day	103
Stand up, stand up, for Jesus	114
Sweetest Name, The	116
Sweet Hour of Prayer	131
Somewhere	136
Sowing Seed for Jesus	138
Seed of The Word of Life	152
Send Out The Life Boat	166
Sowing for the angel reapers	168
Songs of Praise	182
Step Over the Line	172
Trust and Obey	6
Tho' my life-path oft is dreary	19
Thou Shalt Shine	20
Take me by the hand	30
Through The Blood	31
Thou Art My Shepherd	32
There's a sweet, sweet song	48
Thine, Jesus, Thine	74
There's a beautiful country	81
Tell me pilgrim, faint and weary	85
Thro' the meadows green	92
There is Rest in Jesus	94
'Tis All I Need To Know	96
There's a city that looks o'er	111
There is no name	116
To our dear Sabbath school	128
Thou Shalt Hear My Voice	140
Turn, Turn to Him	148
Tell It Out	149
The Great Physician on	51
The Lord of life and glory	84
There is Rest in Jesus	94
Trusting in Thy Promise	169
Tell Jesus	182
'Tis I, Be Not Afraid	115

Title	No.
Up above the stars where the angels dwell	11
Voyage of Life, The	64
Victory March	82
Working for Jesus	187
Watchman of Zion	4
Watchman on the walls of Zion	4
We've Been Redeemed	24
When We All Get Home	41
When I reach the golden shore	43
We are singing songs for Jesus	8
When shining stars their vigils keep	46
W. C. T. U. Song	54
We are sailing o'er an ocean	64
We Should Hear the Angels	78
We are soldiers for Jesus	82
Was there anything	86
When the world is busy	88
Where The Shepherd Leads	92
We'll Gather the Blossoms	93
Wond'rous King	95
We are daughters of a king	95
Who Forgiveth Sins	97
Who is this that forgiveth	97
We're a happy little band	98
We Will Praise His Name	102
When storms around are sweeping	105
We are gliding away	113
Webb	114
When the misty cloud	115
Word for Jesus, A	132
Wake lilies! wake lilies!	134
We are sowing seed for Jesus	138
What is the song of the	141
Would You Know	146
Why Not To-night	150
Webb	151
We Are Coming Home	154
Whatsoever	172
Whiter Than The Snow	179
We are drifting with the tide	180
When thou wakest in the morning	186
What a Crowning	183
We Shall Meet	184
Ye tempted, troubled	57
Ye Are My Witnesses	85
You may know Christ's saving	156

www.ingramcontent.com/pod-product-compliance
Lightning Source LLC
Chambersburg PA
CBHW021727220426
43662CB00008B/736